My Black Hole

An English & Chinese Bilingual Poetry Collection
英语/汉语双语诗集

我的黑洞
My Black Hole

Author: An Yu
Translators: Xela H. and Li Fukang
作者：安遇
译者：西楠，李富康

Published by Salvador Ave. No.5 Indie Publishing House © 2023

ISBN: 9798372600669

first edition

salvador.ave.no5@gmail.com

Authored by An Yu

Translated by Xela H. and Li Fukang

Edited by Noah Rojo

Cover Art by Matt Lawrence (mattlawrence.net)

<u>**About the Author**</u> | 关于作者：

AN YU (安遇), Chinese poet, born in Daying, Sichuan (四川大英) in 1949. He has worked as a farmer, worker, and civil servant of the state, now lives in Chengdu and Beijing (成都-北京). His poetry is in a unique style of its own and doesn't belong to any existing contemporary school of poetry. An Yu is the author of one poetry collection (《后来我们说》) and so on.

安遇，中国诗人，1949 年出生于四川大英。当过农民、工人、国家公务员，现居成都、北京。他的诗风自成一格，并不属于任何已有的当代诗歌流派。著有诗集《后来我们说》等。

<u>**About the Translators**</u> | 关于译者:

Xela H.（西楠）, also known as Xi Nan, writes and translates, indie publisher of *Xi Nan & Fish Lu STUDIO, London*. She recently has been living in Latin America with her life partner.

西楠，写作，翻译，*Xi Nan & Fish Lu STUDIO, London* 工作室独立出版人。她近期和她的爱人旅居拉丁美洲。

**

Li Fukang（李富康）is a poet and poetry translator. His major publications include *Selected Early Poems of Bai Hua* (Scripsi, 1991), *Post-Misty Poetry* (Renditions, 1992), *Salutation To Du Fu by Zhou Sese* (Co-translator, New Century Press, New York, 2019).

李富康，诗人、诗歌译者。主要汉译英作品：《柏桦早期诗选》（澳大利亚，1991 年）；《后朦胧诗选》（香港，1992 年）；《向杜甫致敬：周瑟瑟多语种诗选》（合译，美国，2019 年）。

**

Contents
目录

Chapter I:
Still Old Cohen is Writing Poems
第一章：老科恩还在写诗

An Advanced View

There's a forest in my No Man's Land.

I don't know the names of those trees.

I stand until becoming one of them.

A tree unnamed.

Quiet.

Vibrant. Freckled. I am not sad that autumn begins with me.

晚期风景

有一片森林在我的无人区.

我说不出那些树的名字.

我站成它们中一员.

一棵什么树.

安静.

热烈. 斑驳. 我不悲伤秋天从我开始.

The Toad Prince

My SunSunSunSunSunSun
O Luciano Pavarotti, me too having a sun
in my heart
Me too born with a good voice
Me too having a temporary stage and
a temporary residence permit
Me, a base singer
I'll be singing on

哈莫王子

我的太阳太阳太阳太阳太阳太阳
帕瓦罗蒂啊我心中也有一个太阳
我也有天生一副好嗓子
我也有一个临时舞台和暂住证
我在低音区
我要一直唱下去

Dahlias, Dahlias

So those are dahlias, give me one please. Let me hold it with my
hand
In this way, in this way I'll go back home. Dahlias, dahlias,
let me forget this ageing face of mine for a while.

大丽花，大丽花

那就是大丽花呀，那也给我一枝吧。让我也拿在手
上，就这样，就这样拿在手上回家去。大丽花，大
丽花，让我也忘记自己这张老脸一会儿。

The Dead Sea

Now I see a large cluster of black clouds. And earrings. And Sea
water. I can barely hear
my crying. And yours too. Eh. Woo. Ah. Ya. Die once,
Die twice. I see a large cluster of black clouds. Over and over again.

死海

这时我只看见大团黑云。和耳坠。和海水。我只听
见我的叫喊。也有你的叫喊。嗯。哦。哎。呀。死
一次。又死一次。我看见大团黑云。一次一次。

As You Penetrate, You Start to Gallop

As you madly whip your stump, will, and hip, as you whip
your ugly hip, and its high rise, ugly despair, a piece of grassland
it's your Hulun Buir **(1)**

(1) Hulun Buir (呼伦贝尔) is a region that is governed as a prefecture-level city in

northeastern Inner Mongolia, China. Major scenic features are the high steppes of the Hulun Buir grasslands, the Hulun and Buir lakes (the latter partially in Mongolia), and the Khingan range.

当你深入，开始奔跑

当你拼命抽打你的残腿，意志，和臀部，当你抽打
丑陋的臀部，和它高高耸起的，丑陋的绝望，一块
草地，它就是你的呼伦贝尔。

I'm

I'm caressing her hand, and I know, she's looking at me, just like the moonlight
following a lonely wolf, moving, lighting the wilderness, hills, river valleys.
I dare not to linger even in my dream. I show my ferocious gaze to all.

我在

我在抚摸她的手，而且我知道，她在低眉看我，就像月
光，跟着孤独的狼，在移动，为它照亮旷野，山岗，河
谷。我在自己梦里也不敢久留。我对周遭的目光恶狠狠。

My Horse Head, My Fiddle

February, baby grass budding out of sands.

March, vital and fresh.

April, short skirts.

May went crazy, and you followed.

June came after with no delay.

It was her grassland, and your grassland too?

You stayed with yourself in July.

You went to Qinghai in August. **(1)**

You climbed Mt.Tianshan in September. **(2)**

Was it hers or yours, the sobbing grassland?

Oh, sweet little thing.

(1) Qinghai (青海) is a large, sparsely populated Chinese province spread across the high-altitude Tibetan Plateau. It's a place of strong Tibetan and Mongol cultural traditions.

(2) Mt. Tian Shan (天山), literally meaning the Heavenly Mountain, is a large system of mountain ranges located in Central Asia. The highest peak in the Tian Shan is Jengish Chokusu, at 7,439 metres (24,406 ft) high. Its lowest point is the Turpan Depression, which is 154 m (505 ft) below sea level.

我的马头呢我的琴呢

二月细草穿沙。
三月小清新。
四月短裙子。
五月错乱你跟着错乱。
六月迫不及待。

哎草原是她的也是你的吗。
七月依然孤独。
八月去了青海。
九月翻过天山。
哎草原的呜咽是她的也是你的吗。
小蹄子呀。

Out I'll Go with a Sentence Today

And with only nouns and verbs, only the clean, fresh
and emerging

Like winds through the street, blowing loud on the tree leaves
blowing loud on the flags

Like the girl selling flowers, the village peddler
fluting along the lanes, with their smiling faces

Like me saying "Hi". It's a dictation that guides me
before a sentence happens

今天，我要带着一个句子出门

而且我只要名词和动词，只要干净的，新鲜的
生长的

就像这大街上的风，把那些树叶吹得哗哗哗响

把那些旗子吹得哗哗哗响

就像那个卖花的女孩，那个吹着竹笛走街串巷
的乡村小贩，他们面带微笑

就像我说你好；它是一种旨意，在句子发生前
引领我

Wild Ducks

The wild ducks netted their love on the water, quacking-quacking, flapping their wings. In this teahouse on the water. Friends are talking loudly, while you push open the window, go quacking-quacking after those ducks. You have your own way, thinking you are closer to the free, daring and clean things.

野鸭子

野鸭子在水上收获了爱情，嘎嘎嘎叫，张开翅膀扑扑飞．这
里是水上茶园．朋友们一直在高谈阔论，你推开窗子，跟着
那些鸭子嘎嘎叫．你自以为是，你以为你比他们更接近那些
自由大胆干净的事物．

In This Madding World, I'm Waiting for a Snowfall

Just like me in waiting for someone
joyful
and quiet

thinking that she's here silently
When looking up
occasionally
she's standing right outside the window

icy cold
and warm

这个世界太热闹，我在等一场雪

就像我在等一个人
又欢喜
又安安静静的那种

总以为她悄悄来了
什么时候
一抬头
她就站在窗外

又冰凉
又温暖

On the Levee

I say Hi with the new leaves of this willow twig
I say Goodbye with the new leaves of this willow twig
They too are my new leaves
Every morning when I go for a walk on the levee
I recognize the futility of my intercourse with this spring
Don't you think so
the new leaves in the breeze are me
the new leaves in the drizzle are me

在河堤上

我用这柳枝的新叶向你问好
我用这柳枝的新叶向你告别
它们也是我的新叶
每天清晨我去河堤上走
我认可我与这个春天媾合的无效方式
你不觉得吗
微风中的新叶是我
细雨中的新叶是我

Hanging Red Peppers onto the Wall

Hanging red peppers onto the wall
making them permanent lanterns

Having a happy family life
the dinner table unites us sitting around
With teeth
we analyze the hardness of a supper

One century and one more
as long as you take a firm bite

that's the way we take
that's the way we like

Hosting the dinner table
mother
looks happy

but the peppers
always make us tearful

把辣椒挂在墙上

把辣椒挂在墙上
就是永远的灯笼

做一份好人家
让桌子团结我们坐下来
用牙齿
分析一顿晚餐的硬度

一百年加一百年
只要你一口咬定

这是我们的接受方式
也是我们喜欢的方式

餐桌的主持
母亲
表情幸福

而辣椒
总是催人泪下

Out for Fun

Out seeing a belle
hair uncombed

A schoolboy
schoolbag loaded

A Taiji practitioner **(1)**
self-focused

A tramp on a bench
covered with sunlight

Clear river water
clear river of sands

Willows in the wind
truly willowy

Is that an egret?
Surely it is

I salute to them there
with eyes

I salute to them here
with eyes

Hi, I say
who are you

(1) Taiji（太极）, short for Taiji Quan（太极拳）, sometimes also known as "Shadowboxing", is an internal Chinese martial art practiced for defense training, health benefits, and meditation. Taiji has practitioners worldwide.

出门见喜

美女什么情况
头不梳

小儿读书郎
书包好沉

打太极的人
目中无人

流浪汉睡长椅
阳光如被

沙河水清
才是沙河

风中的柳树
才像柳树

那是白鹭吗
真是白鹭

我向他们
行注目礼

也向它们
行注目礼

我说你好
你是谁

Village Song

A nail flower, is going to the city for love, on her rustic way out
home **(1)**
A drop of water, on the slope of a leaf, is walking to the sea for

crying, not along the river

村歌

一朵指甲花，去城里找爱情，出门就是山路。
一滴水，在叶子的坡度上，到大海去哭，它不沿着河流走。

Afternoon Tea

Saying nothing about youth and decay in time
you are this big ficus virens tree
It says nothing
saying nothing of the conservative party
or liberalism in love stories
You are the wind sitting on tree leaves
No matter when
it enables things around to
shine in the sun
Being still
or in motion
it says nothing

下午茶

不说时光里的青春与衰老
你就是这棵大黄桷树了
它什么都不说
不说爱情故事里的保守党
与自由主义
你就是这坐在树叶上的风了
什么时候
它都可以让身边的事物
在太阳底下闪闪发光
它静止
它大动
什么都不说

Three Small Colored Banners

1. Trying to write a poem in early morning, failed, while seeing daffodils on the windowsill produce some good sentences.
2. Opening the door, the little girl of my neighbor was crying for her mum, her petaled voice wets my whole body.
3. At the elevator entrance, an old man on the wheelchair wears a tattered coat of shame.

三朵小彩旗

1. 清晨写一小诗，不成，看见窗台上的水仙长出了好句子。
2. 开门，邻家女孩在哭，喊妈妈，花瓣儿的声音洒我一身。
3. 电梯口，坐在轮椅上的老人，脸上挂着破布一样的羞愧。

Dao of Mount Qingcheng (1)(2)

Green twigs above
Green mosses under

In between
you may do deep breathing

Deep breathing
Deep breathing

That's it?
That's it

And with her agreeably
on the green slate

(1)   Dao or Tao (道) is the natural order of the universe whose character one's intuition must discern to realize the potential for individual wisdom, as conceived in the context of East Asian philosophy, East Asian religions, or any other philosophy or religion that aligns to this principle.

(2)   Mount Qingcheng (青城山) is a mountain in Dujiangyan, Sichuan, China (中国四川省都江堰市). It is considered one of the birthplaces of Taoism and one of the most important Taoist centres in China.

问道青城山

上有青枝
下有青苔

你在中间
就做深呼吸好了

深呼吸
深呼吸

就这些吗
就这些

青石板上
可以有她

It's Spring, and A Bitter Wife Too

Standing right under the eaves of an old house, she sees
peach blossoms a disease
and rain drops a disease
O Newbridge Town
O Nine Miles Village
What will happen if starting off for a remote place in this spring?
What will happen to the canola flowers on the hillsides?
What will happen to the old people abandoned?

It's spring, and a failed scholar too
It' s the prodigal son
the cold palmed the and pale faced
It's spring, and a pink lady too
She walks in her sorrow
holding a red umbrella, so gorgeous
Wind blowing
flowers falling
water flowing

这是春天，也是怨妇

她就站在老房子的屋檐下
看桃花是一场疾病
看雨水也是一场疾病
新桥镇啊
九里乡啊
这个春天出趟远门会怎样
坡上的油菜花会怎样
留守的老人会怎样
这是春天，也是落榜秀才
失足者
手心冰凉者面色苍白者
这是春天，也是三小姐
她走在她的忧愁里
打红伞，那么美
风在吹
花在落
水在流

Breeze of Spring

Breeze of this spring
blows as it wishes
touching the peach blossom
and being touched as well
Oh, her little lips
on your cheek
make nothing happen

这个春天的风

这个春天的风
怎么吹
桃花都是被动的
也是主动的
她小小的唇啊
在你脸上
你怎么都不是

The Peach Blossom

So that's her, peach blossom, she's about to give away her
frail flesh

I hear in the rain, her vague cry

but it's not the time saying it, but it's the time saying it
I'll take her in my hand, running through the mud of spring

How nice, as she's returning to the eaves of her old home
as I am standing in the shreds of moonlight

So that's her, peach blossom, with her frail cry she
imprisons me

桃花

那就是桃花呀，她就要守不住她
小小的身子了

我在雨水中，分明听见她的叫喊了

但是现在我不能说，但是现在我想说
我要拉着她的手，去春天的泥泞里奔跑

多好啊，当她回到老房子的屋檐下
当我站在月光的碎片里

那就是桃花呀，一声小小的惊叫
困住了我

My Black Hole

First, it's a hymn for the Dead Poets Society that I failed to write.
Then it's my obsession in writing it, beyond death.

我的黑洞

先是一首关于死亡诗社的赞美诗，我不曾写出。
再是我迷恋于写出，超乎死。

Subway

One step back, one more step back, close to
the cliff of time, and you are a moving old house
Her flesh hurts your integrity, ribs and kindness
adding one bite of sight as she turns back
to make you decay faster

地下铁

退后一步，再退后一步，靠边
在时间的悬崖上，你就是一间移动的老房子
她的肉身压痛了你的本分，肋骨，和善良
还要回过头来狠狠挖你一眼
让你速朽

Me in the Routine Pattern

It was the one sitting quiet among them
who, just now, for a while

at the seminar themed "happy life"
left me

I left me, nothing could stop that
neither they, nor a knife

nor the horizon

我在日常秩序中

就是那个坐在他们中间默不作声的人
可是，刚才，有一阵

在幸福生活研讨会现场
我离开了我

我离开我，又有什么拦得住
我看他们不能，刀子不能

地平线也不能

Still Old Cohen is Writing Poems

Then, under the reign of Old Cohen is none but a girl
This morning
the waitress of the restaurant said to him
Dear
So pleased Old Cohen
wrote one more poem

老科恩还在写诗

后来，老科恩的统治就只是一个少女了
今天早上
餐厅的女侍者叫了他一声
亲爱的
老科恩一高兴
又写了一首

** Chapter I is translated by Li Fukang from Chinese into English.*

第一章由李富康汉译英.

24th

Chapter II:
The Final Square is for the Wanderer Alone
第二章：最后的广场是流浪者一个人的

Lotus in the Lotus Field

You also had a paint brush.

Mountains greening and waters rippling under your brush.

You painted a woman named Lotus (荷) twisting her graceful body,

coming from the sound of music made of water.

And singing.

And dancing.

And her water sleeves, the moonlight were all like water.

And turning around.

And moving faster.

A beauty without sorrow or regret.

Sinful?

Pure.

A hundred years of elegance and talent, the paint brush and ink, all

died.

The great master died.

Lotus stands in the lotus field.

Lotus speaks nothing.

荷在荷田

你也有一支笔。
画山山青画水水荡漾。
画一个名叫荷的女子从水做的音乐声中摇摇摆摆而来。
而歌。
而舞。
而水袖如水月光如水。
而转身。
而加速。
无哀无怨的美丽。
邪耶。
无邪。
百年风流笔墨死。
大师死。
荷在荷田。
荷不语。

Empty Mirror

The mirror is like the old words
my Wangchuan River **(1)**

I often throw the mirror on the ground
I can only be angry at myself

But it's just a break in the language
the words are still there

As if a country conquered and a family ruined
look closely, there's still an inch of mountains and rivers

The hometown is lost
there is still a father, and a mother

The woman who loved you
is still a woman

I say, alas, you-
you-

Pick up the words one by one
a broken mirror is still a mirror

Not afraid of seeing today
the fire and ashes of tomorrow

(1) In the Chinese mythology, people after death have to go across the Gate of Hell and the Wangchuan River (忘川河), the river of forgetfulness. There is a Naihe Bridge (奈何桥) over the Wangchuan River, and at the bridge sits an old woman called Grannie Meng (孟婆). To cross the Wangchuan River, one must cross the Naihe Bridge and drink the Soup of Grannie Meng's (孟婆汤) to forget all the events in his/her past life; otherwise, one is not allowed to cross the Naihe Bridge and enter a reincarnation.

空镜子

旧词一样的镜子

我的忘川

我经常摔镜子
我只能生自己的气

但它只是语言的断裂
词还在

犹如国破家亡
细看，还有一寸山河

故乡失守
还有爹在，娘在

爱你的女人
还是女人

我说，你呀
你呀

一个字一个字去捡
破镜子也是镜子

不怕今天
看见明天的大火和灰烬

Back Then

There were big cypress trees, tallow trees, Chinese honey locusts,
magnolia cocos
There was a cemetery, and a stone engraved with the deceased
parents' names
There were deep grass, wild rabbits, weasels and stink snakes
There were stone paths, bushes, wisteria, hornets' nests
There was a well-kept yard
There were lying cows

There was a temple, a little woman went up the mountain to burn
joss sticks
A monk went down the mountain for alms, he walked past
her sideways

There were cuckoos, they sang once
and the woman got up from bed
they sang again, and the man left home

There was a red bridal sedan chair, a small band to welcome the
bride
There was a red head veil, clothes and quilts patterned with big
flowers
There was a daughter next door, married at the age of sixteen or
seventeen

There were mugwort leaves, calamus, realgar wine
The little aunt who came home was sick, sweat at night
There were bamboo shadows on the earthen walls
There was a faint smell of Chinese herb medicine in the air

29th

Afraid of ghosts when it turned dark
they told stories in the moonlit clearing
frightened the kids
frightened themselves, too

There was tranquility
in the skeletons of the flowers and the night

那时

有大柏树，乌桕，皂角，夜合欢
有阴地，有刻着先妣先考的石头
有深草，野兔子，黄鼠狼，菜花蛇
有石板路，灌木，紫藤，马蜂窝
有打扫得很干净的院子
有卧牛

有寺庙，有小妇人上山烧香
僧人下山化缘，他侧着身子
从她身边走过

有布谷鸟，叫一声
女人就起床了
叫一声，男人就出门了

有花轿，有迎亲小乐队
有红盖头，大朵朵花衣裳，花被子
邻家有女，十六七岁就嫁人了

有艾叶，菖蒲，雄黄酒
回家来的小姨妈有病，夜里盗汗
土墙上有竹子影子
空气有淡淡的中药味

天黑了怕鬼
他们在月亮坝里说故事
把小孩吓着了
把自己也吓着了

有宁静
在花朵和黑夜的骨殖里

A Pumpkin, is a Copper Mine

A pumpkin
is a copper mine

Along the green mountains by the pass
mother is ringing yellow bright flowers
all her way down

A day is standing under the tree
that is the day to fly faraway

The messenger
comes from the other side of the mountains

It's getting dark
father's sitting in the pumpkin field and making gold jewelry

Tomorrow, he will put the most beautiful one
on his daughter

一个南瓜，就是一个铜矿

一个南瓜
就是一个铜矿

寻着崖口上的青青余脉
母亲一路敲响
黄亮亮的花朵

树下站着一个日子
是远走高飞的日子

送信的人
从山那边过来

天黑了
父亲坐在南瓜地里打金首饰

明天，把最美丽的那一颗
戴在女儿头上

Father

is like a haystack that has experienced winter
his shadow dwarfs
in the twilight of the fields
gone

Reed bamboos in front of the house, are the sonorous cries of his
sons and daughters
growing
growing, new shoots bursting out of the canes

父亲

像经过冬天的草垛
父亲的影子，在大田的暮色里
矮下去
没了

房前的芦竹，是儿女宏亮的哭声
长起来
长起来，胀破肢节

Last Scene in the Mundane World

To put your hands down, was to put everything down

That day, you were so calm, just like that dusk
amid the green hills and the setting sun, someone was hurrying on
their way before dark
a dog was barking, someone was yelling at her child
to fetch some firewood home. That was the moment.
You made us believe what we saw that day, ever since:
as if you really passed away, with peace of mind

最后的人间

把手放下，就是把什么都放下
那天，你那样平静，就像那个黄昏
在青山落日之中，有人在天黑前匆匆赶路
有狗吠传来，有人大声喝斥孩子
抱柴火回家，就在那个时候
你让我们后来一直相信，那天我们看到的
好像你真的是，放心地走了

Them

Extracts of *Sociological Research of Suicides among Rural Elderly: Calm and Tragic Suicides of Rural Elderly* reported by Xuan Jinxue, a reporter of *China Youth Daily* **(1)**

The Nameless 1

Old man wanted to kill himself

but was afraid that his children wouldn't bury him
so he dug himself a pit
lay in it
covering his own body with soil
while drinking farm chemical

Old Man Chai (柴) Said

Every old person here has three sons:
son Chemical
son Rope
son Water
These three sons are the most reliable **(2)**

The Nameless 2

The old man was critically ill
his son, who was working outside, took time off to return home
Two or three days passed
he found no sign of his father dying
Son asked him:
Are you going to die or not?
I only took seven days off work
including the time for the funeral
The old man then killed himself
and the son rushed to finish the funeral within a week
and returned to the city to continue his work

Lin Muwen (林木文)

After Lin Muwen took a bath
he changed into clean clothes
The 69-year-old man
sat in the middle of the main hall
burning joss papers for himself in the brazier
while drinking half a bottle of farm chemical

The Nameless 3

The old man was paralyzed in bed
End of the year, his children discussed cutting off water, food for
him
hoping that he would die before the end of the year
"So that the house wouldn't stink
when guests visit during the New Year"
The old man didn't want to die
so he lay on the bed, cursing,
grabbing his feces and threw them around
until the first day of the new year
when he breathed his last

The Nameless 4

Someone had difficulties moving around
could neither reach the farm chemical bottle nor stand on the stool
to hang himself
so tied a rope to
the window that was lower than a person's height
hung his head
and curled up the legs

Couple 1

An elderly couple drank the farm chemical to kill themselves at the same time, the old woman died instantly, and the old man didn't die, but they did not send him to a hospital. The next day, the family held a funeral for the old woman and let the old man lie in bed to watch. On the third day, the old man died, and they used the funeral spirit shed for the old woman to hold the funeral for the old man immediately.

Couple 2

The two elderlies couldn't get food from their son and
were repeatedly beaten and scolded by their daughter-in-law
They plunged headfirst
into a water cellar

The Nameless 5

Even before committing suicide
they considered for their children as much as possible
Some of them didn't choose to kill themselves at home
but had chosen a deserted hill slope, or a ditch
or did not kill themselves after an argument with their children
but waited until things calmed down
When two elderlies both wanted to die
they didn't choose a same day
or a same room
but staggered

The villagers were laughing when telling me these in a light-hearted
manner. Sometimes
I feel like escaping, feel that this world
isn't for me

(1) The book *A Sociological Study on the Living Conditions of the Elderly in Rural
Areas* (农村老年人生活状况的社会学研究) is authored by scholar Liu Yanwu (刘
燕舞) and reporter Xuan Jinxue (宣金学) from *China Youth Daily* (中国青年报) has
written a few news reports about the book.
(2) "The three sons" here mean the three ways of suicide: drinking farm chemicals,
hanging oneself and drowning oneself. Some Chinese rural elderly believe that
suicide is a more reliable way to control one's own life and death, rather than relying
on one's own children.

他们

—— 中国青年报记者宣金学报导《农村老年人自杀的
社会学研究：农村老人自杀的平静与惨烈》摘录

无名者 1

老人要自杀
但怕子女不埋他
便自己挖了个坑
躺在里面
边喝农药
边扒土

柴老汉说

我们这儿的老人都有三个儿子
药儿子
绳儿子
水儿子
这三个儿子最可靠

无名者 2

老人病危
在外打工的儿子请假回家
两三天过去
发现父亲没死的迹象
儿子问他
你到底死不死啊
我就请了七天假
是把办丧事的时间算进来的
老人随后自杀
儿子赶在一周内办完丧事
回城继续打工

林木文

林木文沐浴之后
换上一身干净衣服
这个 69 岁的老人
坐在堂屋中间
一边在火盆里为自己烧纸钱

一边喝下半瓶农药

无名者 3

老人瘫痪在床
年底，子女们商量给老人断水，断粮
希望他在年前死掉
"免得过年家里来客人
屋里臭哄哄的"
老人不想死
躺在床上嗷嗷大骂
抓起粪便乱扔
一直坚持到大年初一
才咽下最后一口气

无名者 4

有人因为行动困难
拿不到药水瓶也站不上板凳悬梁
便在不及人高的窗户上
搭起一根绳
挎住头
蜷起腿

夫妇俩 1

一对老年夫妇同时喝农药自尽，老
太太当场死亡，老爷子没死，但他
们不送他去医院，第二天家里人给
老太太办丧事，就让老头躺在床上

看。第三天老头毙命，他们就着为
老太太办丧事的灵棚立马为老头办
了丧事。

夫妇俩 2

两位老人儿子不给饭吃还
屡遭媳妇打骂两人头朝下
扎进水窖中

无名者 5

他们即便自杀还处处为子女着想
他们有的不会在家自杀
而是选择荒坡，河沟
或者与子女争吵后不自杀
待到关系平静后自杀
两个老人都想自杀
也不会选择同一天
或同一屋
而是要错开

学者刘燕舞说

村民嘻嘻哈哈跟你讲这些有时候
有股想逃离的感觉觉得这个世界
不属于我

Didn't Know It was Autumn

Didn't know it was autumn, that was no big deal
Now things are happening one after another, you see, first the spring was here
we didn't know that spring was here, then when turning around and looking up
we were startled by the shorter skirts, and before knowing it, the summer was here
This was no big deal, either, because we were busy hurrying to what was happening today
good things bad things, invitations and phone calls coming in one after another, and there was no way to escape from them
You see, now the autumn is here, we didn't know it was already autumn
only me and you were left arguing in the empty room
Those who had gained, were gone long ago

不知道是秋天了

不知道是秋天了，这不是什么事
现在的事一件接着一件，你看先是春天来了
我们不知道春天来了，后来一转身一抬头
被更短的裙子吓一跳，还没明白过来又是夏天了
这也不是什么事，因为我们正在忙着赶往今天发生的事
好事坏事，请柬和电话一个接一个地来，想躲是躲不开的
你看现在又是秋天了，我们不知道是秋天了
空旷的屋子只剩下我和你争吵不休
有收获的人，他们早走了

Western Window, for X.Q. (1)

There's a rain that keeps falling

Choose to sit in this place- no matter how to look at it, there is an
old-fashioned temperament
The doors and windows are old, tables and chairs are old, the light
is old, so am I
Look at you, still the good of the old days

O, had a few drinks, not much, just slightly drunk, just wanting to
talk, just a twisting tongue

Saying that we were young back then, there wasn't overnight feud
in a quarrel, and that we were in the small town, the days were poor
and hard
I remember the rains the most, watched you go out with an umbrella,
go to the streets, buy groceries, pick up the child
And listening to you complaining, saying that you had a cold, and a
cough

Saying that there was a rain, kept falling

(1) The title "Western Window" (西窗) of this poem was probably inspired
by the poem "Note on a Rainy Night to a Friend in the North" (夜雨寄北)
by the Tang Dynasty poet Li Shangyin (李商隐): "...when shall we be

trimming wicks again, together in your western window..." (何当共剪西窗烛) Now people sometimes use the term "West Window" to refer to the gathering and talking among old friends and family members (in hope and longing).

西窗，给 X.Q.

有一场雨一直在下

选择这个地方来坐，怎么看，都有一种旧日子的气质
门窗是旧的，桌椅是旧的，光线是旧的，我也是
看你也是，旧时的好

哦喝了几杯，也不多，只是微醺，只是想说，只是舌头打转

说那时年轻，吵架没有隔夜仇，我们在小县城，日子清苦
最记得那些雨水，看你打伞出门，上街，买菜，接孩子
听你抱怨，说你有寒，咳嗽

说有一场雨，一直在下

Three Lines on Mid-Autumn Day

1.
Under the moonlight, don't just sit and let yourself become a cloud

of shadow
The Creator doesn't take sides, and tonight you have as many silver coins as they do
Follow the road back out, and you'll be saved

2

Today I've just drawn a circle on the paper
I've just drawn the rear views of two persons sitting head-to-head in the circle
The person on the right, is reaching up and pointing to the sky

中秋三句

1

月光下，你不要把自己坐成一团阴影
天地不仁，今夜你也有他们一样多的银币
从出来的路上往回走，你就得救了

2

今天我只是在纸上画了一个圆
只是在圆里画了两个人头挨头坐在一起的背影
右边那个人，伸手指着天上

**At the Studying Pavilion of Chen Zi'ang's,
I Saw His Rear View Standing on the Cliff Overlooking (1)**

Invasion from the North, invasion from the North, how can I read in peace? Shangguan Style, Shangguan Style, Shangguan Style again, how can I read in peace? **(2)** The flood of the Fu River (涪江) turned a corner in the front, rushed to the foot of the mountain and made a half-circle, stopped for a moment, or maybe not. Alas, this biting midge, this biting midge, how can I read in peace, how can I read in peace?

(1)   Chen Zi'ang (陈子昂) was a Chinese poet of the Tang dynasty (唐代).

(2)   Shangguan Style (上官体) was a poetry style in the Tang Dynasty. It was a kind of palace poetry represented by poet and politician Shangguan Yi (上官仪). Chen Zi'ang was known for opposing the Shangguan Style.

在陈子昂读书台，我看见他站在崖上远眺的背影

北方入侵，北方入侵，这书怎么读。上官体，上官体，还是上官体，这书怎么读。涪江河的大水在前面拐了个弯，冲到山脚下绕半圈，停了一下，又像没停。嗨这墨墨蚊，这墨墨蚊，这书怎么读，这书怎么读。

\

The One Who Knows the Answer Went Far; a Tribute to Yang Li (1)

That man stood in the wind
shouted loudly across the river
shouted loudly

Shouted loudly, shouted loudly

What was he shouting?

A unsettled small case of Modern Chinese poetry
is screwed up in my hand

(1) The background of the above poem is the famous Chinese poem "Loudly" (《大声》) authored by poet Yang Li (杨黎), in which Yang Li wrote: "We were standing by the river / shouting loudly to the person across the river / ...He was walking from the river / into the distance..." (我们站在河边上 / 大声地喊河对面的人 / ……他正从河边 / 往远处走……)

知道的那个人走远了，致敬杨黎

那人站在风中
朝着河对岸大声喊
大声喊

大声喊，大声喊

他在喊什么呢

一个新诗的小案件
砸在我手里

Wide Road is a Black Music for the Blind

The wide road is a black music for the blind
lifting the running world up and down gently
It's dark now, and someone's reading an advert under the streetlight
someone's singing at the beer stall:
O, the sea, the sea
O, the sea, the sea
The road is leading people under the tongue root of the sea

大路是一支黑色的盲人音乐

大路是一支黑色的盲人音乐
把奔跑的世界轻轻托起又放下
天黑了，有人在路灯下看广告
有人在啤酒摊唱歌
大海呀大海
大海呀大海
路在大海的舌根底下牵着人走

Amsterdam

Stone house of the Dutch pirates, the old face of Amsterdam
you can't go deeper

The origin of this glass of fresh milk in the hand, a pasture where
you don't see the edge or cattle and sheep

you can't go deeper

Goldfish are swimming towards you in the light, there is a kind of transparency
you can't go deeper

阿姆斯特丹

荷兰海盗的石头房子，阿姆斯特丹的昔日表情
你无法深入

手中这杯鲜奶的源头，看不到边际也看不到牛羊的牧场
你无法深入

灯光下的金鱼游向你，有一种透明
你无法深入

Little Rock

Several girls are dancing on the platform at the entrance of the mall, twisting their bodies and twisting.
Michael Jackson was grabbing his crotch on TV, thrusting his hip and thrusting.
A tinker is pounding this off-season in the front street shop, hammering and hammering.
An old female ragpicker is searching in the trash downstairs, poking and poking.

Pigs driven towards the slaughterhouse are walking slowly on the street, tails wagging and wagging.

The juggler with his monkey is beating a gong around the yard, dang-dang-dang-dang.

The pile-driver is striking directly the countryman's heartbeat, thump, thump, thump.

Sounds are falling into dust, handful by handful.

小摇滚

几个女孩子在商场门口的台子上跳舞，一扭一扭。
迈克尔·杰克逊在电视机里手抓裤裆，一挺一挺。
补锅匠在前街边铺子里敲打淡季，一锤一锤。
拾荒的老妇人在楼下的垃圾桶里寻找，一戳一戳。
赶去屠宰场的猪在街上慢走，尾巴一甩一甩。
耍猴戏的人敲着小锣在场子里转圈，当当当当。
打桩机直接击打乡下人的心跳，咚，咚，咚。
声音落进尘土，一把一把。

Art Class

She draws and erases, erases and draws, the street, green trees in front of the tall buildings

The teacher looks at her for a while, speaks nothing, walks away

It's a bit like them, digging both sides of the street again and again changing the street trees again, and again

The teacher teaches the art class, equals to playing
They dig the streets, and she draws the beautiful city, just like playing

O, she's the little girl, Wang Ke (王可), while they, are the big guys, the big company

美术课

她把高楼前面的街道，绿树，画了擦，擦了画
老师看她一会儿，不说话，走开

这有点像他们，把街道两边挖了一次又挖一次
行道树换了一次，又换一次

老师开美术课，等于玩
他们挖街道，她画美丽城市，约等于玩

哦，她是小女孩王可，他们，是大人物，大公司

u Coffee: No Theme Discussion
- take the tree outside the window as an example

The wind and the tree discuss about the direction, the wind is right
The location and the tree discuss about the position, the location is right

The lumberjack and the tree discuss about the lines, the lumberjack
is right
Regarding the questions we are discussing today
take the tree outside the window as an example
I talk to you only
the matter of attitude

u 咖啡：无主题讨论会
　　　　——*以窗外那棵树为例*

风和树讨论方向问题，风是对的
地方和树讨论立场问题，地方是对的
伐木者和树讨论路线问题，伐木者是对的
今天我们讨论的问题
以窗外那棵树为例
我和你们
只说态度问题

Because, Because

Flow breaks in March
riverbed bared

Because of a gust of wind
because of a big rock

Because of an ancient seed

because of a rain

A little flower is
blooming on the riverbank

Because June July August are still far
the floods are still far

Ah, this little joy
A flower is
blooming on the riverbank

因为，因为

三月断流
河床裸露

因为一阵风
因为一块大石头

因为一粒久远的种子
因为一场雨

一朵小花
开在河滩

因为六月七月八月还远
洪水还远

小小的欢乐啊

一朵花
开在河滩

In Spring, a Line Moves a Little

Moves a little on the bank of a pool of peach blossoms
Moves a little in the heart of the river valley that the distant
mountain is reaching into
Moves a little in the place I choose to lie down
Moves a little in an imaginary event
Moves a little in the black abyss and the starry sky
Moves a little in the swirling lights and the mirror
Moves a little where the fingertip touches the palm
Moves a little where the blind cannot see
Moves a little where the mute cannot speak

春天，一根线条移动了一点点

在一泼桃花水的岸边移动了一点点
在远山倾向河谷的腹地移动了一点点
在选择躺下来的地方移动了一点点
在一个假想的事件里移动了一点点
在黑色的深渊和星空里移动了一点点
在旋转的灯光和镜子里移动了一点点
在手心和指尖的触摸处移动了一点点
在瞎子看不见的地方移动了一点点
在哑巴说不出来的地方移动了一点点

Balcony of the Kitchen

Stop going out rashly, binge drinking with friends, bullshitting, bul-
-lshitting about Babel, the Creator doesn't take sides, Babel, or, the rise
and fall of an empire, because of bullshitting, bullshitting, God
naturally doesn't smile, and people are as light as shadows

On the balcony are the washing machine, drying rack, mop, vegetable
basket, stool, ashtray, sitting here for long, and a
word has the chance to come back to life, as the tree outside the window,
sometimes a dead branch, sometimes a new leaf

Can't remember when this started: I'm here

厨房阳台

不再轻易出门，跟朋友烂酒，废话，废
话巴别尔，天地不仁巴别尔，或者，一
个帝国的兴亡，因为废话，废话，上帝
自然不笑，人就轻得像影子

阳台上放着洗衣机，晾衣架，拖布，菜
篮，小凳，烟灰缸，坐这里久了，一个

词就有了复活的可能，像窗外那棵树，
有时一节枯枝，有时一片新叶

不记得什么时候开始的了：我待在这里

Dumb, Dumb, You Come Here

Dumb, dumb, you come here
let's take a picture together

Right under the fence
the stone fence is good

A stone is just a stone anywhere
Beautiful scenery is
neither here nor there

It appears when you don't gesture
when I shut my mouth

哑巴哑巴你过来

哑巴哑巴你过来
我俩合个影

就在围墙下边吧
石头围墙好

石头在哪里都是石头
好风景
不在这里那里

在你不打手势
我把嘴闭上

A New Year is not A New Bride

We just pretend not to know each other.
We just pretend we met but now.
I have just greeted her into the room.

新年不是新娘

只是我们假装不认识．
只是我们假装刚认识．
只是我把她迎进屋了．

Like a Relative

Every day after dinner
when I go downstairs for a walk in the community

always run into him
This man
just like me
always walks with his head down
Does he live in the same block as me?
Don't know
Walk past each other as I lift my eyelids
This person is
a bit like a relative-
when I don't see him
he doesn't exist in my heart
when I do
we both think of our own things

像一个亲戚

每天晚饭后
下楼去小区散步的时候
总会碰见他
这个人
跟我一样
总是低着头走路
他和我在同一个单元吗
不知道
抬眼就过去了
这个人
有点像一个亲戚
不见到
就没这个人
见到了

也是各有各的心事

And the Way She Says No

She blinks
in my naps

She dances happily
in my air

And the way she says no

She doesn't know that she's so little
so little like a preschool girl
so little like five thousand years ago

She doesn't know how beautiful she is
I know that
even watching her weep
would be beautiful

还有她说不的样子

她在我的午睡里
眨眼睛

她在我的空气中

快乐舞蹈

还有她说不的样子

她不知道她那么小
学龄前那么小
五千年前那么小

她不知道她有多美
我知道
看她流泪
也是美的

Thank You, Thank You

But I can't keep you for a while
You aren't here
at the breakfast table
You're not a full stop
in the flowing events
The tree full of pear flowers outside the window
let the rain linger for longer
That is not you
And I'm always with them, them, them, them
What are they talking about?
Now well
I go back to my heart

I close the door

谢谢你，谢谢你

但是我留不了你一会儿
早餐桌上
你不在
川流不息的事件中
你不是一个句号
窗外那树梨花
让雨水有了更多的停留
那不是你
而我总是和他们在一起，他们，他们，他们
他们在说些什么
现在好了
我回到我内心
我把门关上

There's No One There

There's no one there
but you

A drop of birdsong
could
empty you

A drop of water falling into water
could
melt you

What you're taught there
is:
you forget about yourself

and: you're free
as a tree

那里一个人也没有

除了你
那里一个人也没有

一滴鸟鸣
可以
掏空你

一滴水珠落水
可以
化开你

那里教给你的
是
你不在

是你一棵树那样
自在

At This Moment

I want to hold your hands tightly

I want to believe in God
I want to believe in the state
my government
the army

I want to believe in me
I want to

believe in a drop of water
a drop of blood

believe that even a soft cry
can reach

在这个时候

我要紧紧拉住你的手

我愿意相信上帝
我愿意相信国家
政府
军队

我愿意相信我
我愿意

相信一滴水
一滴血

相信轻轻的一声呼唤
也能到达

Hollow

That's it for now
Hang yourself on the net
a black dot
only watch the sky
leave no words
move when wind blows
There are water droplets after rain
sparkling
Seeing a hollow-
that is
inside your heart

破洞

现在就这样了吧

把自己挂在网上
一个黑点
只观天象
不留言
吹风动一下
雨后有水珠
亮晶晶
看得见破洞
那也是
你心中的

You're Startled by Your Knock on the Door

There's a teardrop, that you don't want others to see

There's a stone that you can't throw away

You know a teardrop won't work, and neither will a stone

You know a flower will do

You're not sure you are a flower

你被你的敲门声吓一跳

有一滴眼泪，你不要别人看见

有一块石头你扔不出去

你知道泪水不行，石头也不行

你知道花朵行

你不确定你是花朵

From Anyang to Luoyang, to Gongyi, My Acceleration (1)

The big problem is, sometimes I know a little, not much
The problem is, "when I walk along with two others, they may
serve me as my teachers." **(2)** The problem is
they act like they know everything

(1) Anyang, Luoyang and Gongyi (安阳, 洛阳, 巩义) are all city
names in Henan Province (河南省), China. They're probably on the
same railway line.
(2) This quote is from Confucius (孔子): "When I walk along with
two others, they may serve me as my teachers. I will select their
good qualities and follow them, their bad qualities and avoid them."
(三人行，必有我师焉。择其善者而从之，其不善者而改之。)

从安阳到洛阳，到巩义，我的加速度

大问题是，有时我知道一点，不多
问题是三人行必有我师焉，问题是
他们什么都知道

Yangjia Bridge (杨家桥)

Water has flowed through three autumns, what does it mean?

O, those who said goodbye haven't gone far.
Who's retelling in the wind, some sad stories.
Locust tree leaves are rustling, cannot be stopped.
A stone rests on the stone bridge.
I see you in the water.

杨家桥

水过三秋说的什么意思．
告别的人儿走得不远呐．
谁在风中复述有些伤心事．
槐树叶哗哗哗响停不下来．
石头桥上歇一石头．
我在水中看见你．

Wangwuli Village (1)

Go out of the town entrance, there is the Shuimo River (水磨河),
cross the Gaojia Bridge (高家桥)
go down the path on the left, and climb over the small hill, there is
the Luojiawan (罗家湾) Village

This is an old geographical name: Wangwuli
On the extension of a rudimentary road, a figure is moving

That man walks so slowly, as slow as my grandparents, my parents
walked through their whole life in Wangwuli, and ended up just like

this, slow, small

That man walks so slowly, as slow as me, forever on the way
returning home
moving one single step, a hundred years have passed

As slow as the spring breeze, as distant encomiums and lies
blow on the earth

(1) Wangwuli (望五里), literally means "overlooking five miles", is a village under
the jurisdiction of Hebian Town, Daying County, Suining City, Sichuan Province,
P.R.China (中国四川省遂宁市大英县河边镇下辖行政村).

望五里

出小镇场口，就是水磨河，过高家桥
上左边小路，翻坡就是罗家湾了

这是一个古老的地域名：望五里
在一条土公路的延长线上，移动着一个人影

那个人走得太慢了，慢得像我的祖辈，我的父母
在望五里走完一生，最后也是这样，缓慢的，渺小的

那个人走得真慢啊，慢得像我，永远在回家路上
移动一步，已是百年

慢得像春天的风，像久远的颂词和谎言
在大地吹拂

Hebianchang Town (1)

With water as a neighbor, burning joss sticks for the god of earth on
the back slope
is already climbing high

All their lives they have walked in a low region
always looking for a fulcrum to hang their shoes for air-dry, and
their thoughts
pointing fingers at each other, discussing life

Further up, further up
they sometimes shout and tear at the height of a wine glass
united as brothers seeing long lost brothers

(1) "Hebianchang" (河边场), literally means "the riverside field", is a town located
in Suining, Sichuan Province, China (河边场镇位于中国四川省遂宁市).

河边场

以水为邻，到后坡的土地庙烧柱香
就是一次登高了

他们一生在低处行走
总是在寻找支点晾晒鞋子和思想
互相指责，讨论生活

再往上走，再往上走
他们有时会在一个酒杯的高度叫喊，流泪
团结得像兄弟，看见失散的兄弟

Matou Village, Matou Village, a Part of the Road on Water (1)

There was wind on the water, called memories, called March, slowly blowing, keeping a kind of low-key beauty.
There was an angel on the water, called innocence, called puppy love, who dropped and broke a small mirror.
There were light-inked landscapes on the water, the rivers and mountains; there was a poem on the water, written in wrong grammar.

(1) "Matou" (马头), literally means "horse head", is a village under Daying County, Suining, Sichuan Province, China (马头乡隶属于中国四川省遂宁市大英县).

马头乡，马头乡，有一节路在水上

水上有风，叫回想，叫三月，徐徐保持着低美。
水上有天使，叫无心，叫初心，摔坏了小镜子。
水上有淡墨山水，叫江山，水上有诗，叫病句。

Qikou Town (郪口镇) (1)

Qikou Town, three hundred and three meters above the sea level
Walking on the mountain roads, he would look at the Qi River (郪
江) on the left and the Fu River (涪江) on the right
Traveling via the waters, he would look at the dark pine forest on
the Mingyue Mountain (明月山)
For people who had left hometown, climbing up and gliding down
were both flying

The juvenile without enough money was excited by the old
"jianghu" stories **(2)**, and he pushed the window and shouted
He said he was the robber from the old dynasty, and was coming
down from the mountain
seeing on the dock, the unmarried daughter of an unknown
dignitary standing in the wind
and the penniless scholar bowing and bidding farewell on the fore

As I walked out of the teahouse, things were happening in the dusk
of the town
like money, love and blood
and those I was not sure about

(1) Qikou Town (郪口镇) once belonged to Sichuan Province, China, was revoked in
2019, and its administrative area is now placed under the jurisdiction of Huima Town
(回马镇). Huima Town now belongs to Daying County, Suining City, Sichuan
Province, China (回马镇现隶属于中国四川省遂宁市大英县).
(2) Jianghu (江湖) is the community of martial artists in "wuxia" stories and, more
recently, outlaw societies like the Triads. "Wuxia" (武侠), which literally means
"martial heroes", is a genre of Chinese fiction concerning the adventures of martial
artists in ancient China.

郪口镇

郪口镇，海拔三百零三米
走山路他会看一看左边的郪江右边的涪江
走水路他会看一看明月山的黑松林
离家出走的人，向上攀援向下滑行
都是一次飞翔

不够盘缠的少年被旧时的江湖故事激动，推窗大叫
他说他就是前朝那个劫匪，正从山上下来
看见码头上，谁家的小姐站立风中
落难的秀才揖别船头

走出茶楼，小镇的黄昏正在接近钱财之类
爱情之类和血迹之类
我不确定的事物

Rapeseed Flowers on both Sides of the Qi River (郪江)

Rapeseed flowers on both sides of the Qi River, blossom so lively
every year, like the market on the square
where everyone is splendid, everyone applauds together

Among them, girls like Ying and Fang, have their rapeseed-like
love
and rapeseed-like endings; their little secrets in heart--

blossom here and there as well: like in mornings and afternoons, in front of the Lichun Courtyard **(1)**
girls laughing and having fun, standing straight, shouting, some late, some absent

(1) "Lichun Courtyard" ("丽春园"，亦作"丽春院") was said to be the residence of Su Qing (苏卿), a famous courtesan in the ancient times, and later became the common name for residences of geisha or brothels.

鄞江两岸的油菜花

鄞江两岸的油菜花，年年开得这样热闹，像广场上的集会
每个人都灿烂，大家一起鼓掌

他们中间，小英，小芳这样的女孩子，油菜花一样的爱情
油菜花一样的结果，她们小小的心事

零零星星的也开：像丽春院门口，午前午后的班前会
嘻闹，立正，叫喊，有人迟到，有人缺席

Luojiawan Village (罗家湾)

Those people got some news from the city, left their hoes and went away
so fast, forgetting the dirty aprons and potato baskets, in the soil

Without the slightest hesitation, took nothing with them, but their identities
and left nothing behind, but the old houses, and the gods guarding the gates

The rest, mountains were called green mountains, clouds were called white clouds,
and the childhood was as quiet as the Chinese characters

罗家湾

那些人得到城里一点消息，丢下锄头就走了
他们走得快，把黑围裙和土豆筐，也忘在土里了

没有半点犹豫，他们除了身份，什么也没带走
除了老房子，门神，什么也没留下

剩下这些，山叫青山，云叫白云，静如汉语的
童年

Shima Village · Luo Dufu's Manor (石马乡 · 罗都复庄园)

Like the old landowners in the old days, who fought with silence
confronting stormy revolutions
but their hearts were completely defeated

Stepping through its thick and heavy gates, you read a hundred

answers and a thousand questions
of a family

Granitic foundation, old-fashioned earth-walled houses, the glory
and sin of this former empire
All the questions are gone now

Looking back today
descendants of the old landowners were walking in the ranks of the
revolutionaries.

石马乡·罗都复庄园

像当年的老地主在疾风暴雨的革命面前，以沉默抗衡
而内心完全败落

从它厚重的大门跨进去，你可以读到一个家族的一百个答案
和一千个问题

麻条石地基，老式的土墙房子，昔日黄土帝国的光荣与罪恶
现在所有的问题都没有了

老地主的子孙在革命者的队伍中行走，今天回过头来
近看是这样，远看还是这样

Pingle, I'm Going to Stay Here Tonight (1)

A man drags his shadow, along the blue stones paved on the old
street
walks past the stores one by one

Finds an inn by the river, makes tea, smokes a cigarette
let the occasional bird chirping, empty the heart

Goes out in the dark, asks about a tavern
finds a seat by the window and sits down

Caravans of the old days, carrying the tea and salt business
went far

Tonight, I'm going to stay here
let the tranquility of the old town and my soul, integrate

(1) Pingle (平乐), a county in Qionglai, Sichuan Province (四川省
邛崃市), China.

平乐，今夜我要在这里住下来

一个人拖着影子，从老街的青石板上走过
从一家一家店铺门前走过

找一家临江的客栈，泡茶，抽烟
让偶尔一声鸟鸣，把心里排空

天黑出门，打听一家小酒馆
找个靠窗的位置坐下

当年的马帮，驮着茶叶生意和盐巴生意
走远了

今夜，我要在这里住下来
和古镇的安宁，做灵魂的生意

Remain

Nobody leaves any remain
and so do you
Even though you have other records
proving
you own small praises
and consolations
Endow the boundless landscape with several nouns (not monument,
not the ever-changing world) and verbs
How many words
become remain

剩余

没有人有剩余
你也一样
即使你有另外的记录
证明你
有小小的赞美
和安慰

赋予无尽山水几个名词（不是纪念碑，不是白云苍狗）和动词
有几个词
成为剩余

A French Movie

On the grass after rain, a snail, is crawling towards another snail.
Le nozze di Figaro sonata is reverberating throughout the world.

法国电影

雨后草地，一只蜗牛，爬向另一只蜗牛。
费加罗的婚礼奏鸣曲响彻整个世界。

The Lover

It's not the first time you are wounded

and she also has a fracture

like a clay pot

still in your grasp

can't keep your hands off her

crazy, beautiful, dangerous

Once it hits the ground, you may not be able to pick it up again

but you still don't want to stop spinning
and dance in the backlight
A kind of giddiness is what you want

You lift your gaze ever higher, and higher
deep in the sky
hiding her

And then, letting her fall in the no-man's grassland
fall, in your waving
o, she is still a flower

情人

你不是第一次受伤
她也有了破损
像一只陶罐
还在你的掌握之中
上下其手
疯狂，美丽，危险

只要一落地，就有可能捡不起来
但你还是不想停止旋转
这样在逆光中舞蹈
要的就是一种玄晕

你把自己的目光不断抬高，抬高
在天空深处
把她藏匿起来

然后，让她在无人的草地落下来
落下来，她在你的挥舞中
还是一朵花呀

The Aesthetics of Lust

Reaching out
you were about to touch her body

And then
the hand paused in the air

And then
the disease was rooted

Imagine a juvenile boy
was under a peach tree

You are more beautiful than he
standing in the wind

偷，不如偷不着

一伸手
就要触摸到她的身体了

接着

手在空中停顿了一下

接着
就落下了病根

假设一个少年
在桃子树下

你比他
站在风中还美

Speed

I turn myself into a bullet
I shoot myself out
and hit her
I've known her for half a minute
I've had this thought my whole life
I was seventeen or eighteen
I was awake
The spring was awake
Ah, what a long time
A seventeen or eighteen-year-old beautiful boy walked along the riverbank
A seventeen or eighteen-year-old bad boy climbed over the courtyard wall
She came from the opposite

I turned myself into a bullet

and shot out

Faster than

those who sang love songs on the riverbanks full of verdant reeds in

the days of Shijing **(1)**

Faster than

on the ninth page of a thick book

when Childe Jia (贾公子) first saw the schoolgirl Sister Lin (林妹

妹) **(1)**

(1) *Shijing* (诗经), the Classic of Poetry, is the oldest existing collection of Chinese poetry, comprising 305 works dating from the 11th to 7th centuries BC. And "a thick book" in the penultimate line here probably refers to *Dream of the Red Chamber* (红楼梦), a novel composed by Chinese writer Cao Xueqin (曹雪芹) in the middle of the 18th century. Overall, the poet is probably attempting to present the slow-paced love of the ancients in the last six lines of this poem, as a comparison to nowadays.

速度

我把我变成一颗子弹

我把我打出去

击中她

我认得她有半分钟了

我有这个想法已经一生一世了

我十七八岁

我已经苏醒

春天已经苏醒

多漫长的时光啊

十七八岁的美少年走过河堤

十七八岁的坏小子翻过院墙

她从对面走来
我把我变成一颗子弹
打出去
比诗经时代在蒹葭苍苍的河岸唱情歌的人
快一点
比在一本厚书的第九页
贾公子第一眼见到女学生林妹妹的时候
快一点

First Quarter Moon

I say I'm lying in an inn, I'm lying at home, I'm lying
in the haystack, I mean the same thing

Whenever, I say I'll wait for you for an hour, for ten days or half a
months
I am saying that, I'll wait for you for a thousand years

I see me lying down, with my head resting on the north, my
forehead desolate, like a desert
hopeless, far away

I see you quietly coming out, drifting out, the half face pure and
noble
lightening me up, and the mountains and waters of the mundane
world

I see you leaning down, slightly bowing your head, long hair
covering your face
long hair covering me, and a small window, a hut

A person in an alien land, a person on the road, haystacks, in my
childhood

I say I like to, see you drifting out, I say I'll wait
to see you bow your head, I mean the same thing

上弦月

我说我躺在客栈，我说我躺在家中，我说我躺在
干草堆里，一个意思

什么时候，我说等你一个时辰，等你十天半月
那都是在说，等你千年

我看见我躺下去，头枕北方，前额荒凉，如大漠
绝望，辽远

我看你悄然出来，飘然出来，玉洁冰清半张脸
照亮我，人间山水

我看你俯下身来，轻轻一低头，长发遮你脸
长发覆盖我，小窗，小屋

人在他乡，人在路上，干草堆，在我童年

我说我喜欢，看你飘然出来，我说我等待

看你那一低头，一个意思

The Final Square is for the Wanderer Alone

The ex-little-lover's heart was higher than the sky
but still he climbed up again and again
and picked for her stars and gems

Awakened up by a jolt of cold

The final square, half-moon, frail, ancient, beautiful lies and a sickle

最后的广场是流浪者一个人的

昔日的小恋人心比天高
但他还是一次次翻上去
给她摘了星星宝石的

一个激灵冷醒了的

最后的广场，半个月亮，虚弱，古老，谎言镰刀美

Man Under Tree

A man is under a tree
sitting
two hands
holding the void
His gaze is falling off inch by inch
in the distance
Faraway mountains
river valleys
villages
lawns
varied flowers
and the long-ago things
the people close to him
in his heart
darkened
tightened
and some black cryptic words
A stone
by the side
sitting
holding
more tightly than he holds himself

一个人在树下

一个人在树下
坐着
两手空空
抱着
目光在远处

寸寸脱落
远山
河谷
村寨
草坪
纷繁的花
及至久远的事
亲近的人
在他的内心
转暗
收紧
及至黑色的隐语
一块石头
在边上
坐着
抱着
比他把自己抱得更紧

Story of the Stones

Stones, stones, later only two were left. The ones that remain
in my memory today are: one by Carlos Andrade, from Brazil--in
the
middle of the road, there is a stone; the other is from Poland,
Zbigniew
Herbert--someone is inside the stone, looking at you with clear eyes.
(1)

(1) Carlos Drummond de Andrade (1902-1987) was a Brazilian poet. Zbigniew Herbert (1924-1998) was a Polish poet.

石头记

石头，石头，后来就剩下了两块，今天还留在
我的记忆里，一块卡洛斯的，来自巴西，在路
中央，有一块石头，另一块来自波兰，赫贝特
的，有人在石头里面，拿清澈的眼晴看你。

I've Been to the Memorial Temple of Sir Jia in Changjiangba (1)

Just a small house by the roadside. There was nothing inside, only an old woman
received me. She looked like the kind of person who retired as a village cadre, saying things like there was no money for development here. Understood what she meant, gave her some money, then she lit a joss stick, made you stand straight, and listen to her mumbling and praying for you. Late, when walking on the riverbank, you suddenly thought that the name Jia Dao (贾岛) was actually desolate, you saw your shadow very desolate.

(1) Memorial Temple of Sir Jia (贾公祠, Sichuan), located at Changjiangba, Daying County, Suining, Sichuan, China (中国四川遂宁市大英县长江坝), was built to commemorate Jia Dao (贾岛), a famous poet in the Tang Dynasty (唐代).

长江坝贾公祠我去看过了

就路边一间小房子。里面什么也没有，只一老妇人
迎着。看样子她是退下来的村干部那种人物，说些
这里没钱搞开发之类的话。听懂了她的意思，给点
钱，她就燃一炷香，拉你站好，听她念念有词为你
祈福。后来去河岸上走，你会突然想起贾岛这个名
字本来就荒凉，你看见你的影子很荒凉。

The Distance

Disasters caused by wars, heavy rains, floods, diseases, aging,
poverty, and almost no food
The summer of Year 770, at the age of fifty-nine, Du Fu was still
stucked in the area of Leiyang and could not get out **(1)**
Actually he also knew, such tossings were only dying struggles
and Du Fu was still just Du Fu. In the end
on the boat, he was writing poetry **(2)**

(1) Leiyang（耒阳）is now a county-level city and the third most populous
county-level division in Hunan Province, China. Leiyang is under the administration
of the prefecture-level city of Hengyang.
(2) Du Fu (杜甫) was a Chinese poet and politician of the Tang dynasty. Along with
his elder contemporary and friend Li Bai (李白), he is frequently called the greatest
of the Chinese poets. His greatest ambition was to serve his country as a successful
civil servant, but he proved unable to make the necessary accommodations.

远方

兵乱，大雨，洪水，疾病，衰老，穷困，眼看断炊
770 年夏，五十九岁的杜甫还在耒阳一带转不出去
其实他也知道，这样折腾就是玩命
而杜甫也只是杜甫，最后了
在船上，他在写诗

Chapter II is translated by Xela H. from Chinese into English.

第二章由西楠汉译英.

- The End | 完 -